To Fiona
xoxo
Yvette

Merry Christmas
2017!
Colleen, Emily & Izzy

Entertain Effortlessly
Gift Deliciously

VERSATILE RECIPES FOR
ENTERTAINING
AND
GIFT GIVING

Yvette Jemison

YDelicacies.com
y_delicacies Instagram
YDelicacies Pinterest

To Skip, Christine and Adrienne,

There isn't anything that I would rather do than to get in the kitchen, whip up delicious treats, and enjoy them in your company.

XOXO
Yvette

Contents

Recipe Index

*Herb
Marinated Feta p.16*

*Feta
Palmiers p.19*

*Roasted Grape and
Feta Tart p.20*

*Pistachio
Honey p.28*

*Pistachio
Thyme Dip p.31*

*Pear &
Ricotta Tart p.32*

Strawberry Jam p.40

*Strawberry Poppy
Seed Cake p.43*

*Chocolate Chunk
Meringues with
Strawberry Drizzle p.44*

Bacon Jam p.52

*Bacon Jam &
Mushroom Hand Salad p.55*

Bacon Jam Quiche p.56

*Pear Salad with Bacon
Jam Vinaigrette p.59*

*Candied Thyme
Pecans p.66*

*Roasted Acorn Squash with
Candied Thyme Pecans p.69*

*Cheese Board with Candied
Thyme Pecans p.70 & Candied
Pecan Goat Cheese Roll p.71*

*Chicken Salad with
Candied Thyme Pecans p.73*

Holiday Biscotti p.80

Holiday Biscotti
Semifreddo p.83

Sweet and Savory
Scones p.88

Lemon Blueberry
Scones p.90

Asiago & Sun Dried
Tomato Scones p.93

Glitter Cookies p.100

Mookie Cookies p.103

Foreward

By Gary Darling
New Orleans Chef of the Year
Owner/Partner: Zea Rotisserie & Grill, Semolina,
Mizado Latin Kitchen, TasteBuds

In the past forty-five years as a professional chef, restaurateur, and culinary instructor, I have collected an eclectic library of books on the subject of cuisine. The authors range from world renown celebrity chefs, junior leagues, food technologists, food critics, culinary historians and philosophers. Each and every one of them opened a door into the world of the author. They brought to life the history, culture, local food sources, cooking techniques, and cookware needed to provide the meals for family and friends. In my opinion, good cookbooks should never be just a random collection of recipes, they should also reflect the heart and soul of the author. Good cookbooks are stories about the flavors, aromas, textures, and the events that take place at dinner tables. They are memories and reflections of exotic travel; they elevate that moment in life that we experience a unique combination of ingredients with a flavor that we will never forget. They are the memories from our youth that preserve our family history. Think about the aroma of cinnamon baking in your mother's kitchen. I can't shake that memory from my mind. A good cookbook is a gift for a lifetime.

Enough said about my passion for collecting cookbooks, however, I would like to take the time to talk about Yvette Jemison and her first book "Entertain Effortlessly, Gift Deliciously".

I have had the pleasure of her friendship for over thirty years. I have a great deal of respect for this woman of enormous talent in multiple creative disciplines. As a trained speech pathologist, world traveler, potter, writer and photographer, she always pursued her passion with a culinary commitment. As a friend, I have been the recipient of her creative delectables and marvel at her energy to continue to challenge herself. As a speech pathologist she incorporated cooking classes to help her clients in their therapy. That is the level of her culinary curiosity. Her book offers the reader base recipes that are then extended into various appetizers, tarts, salads, savory and sweet confitures that lend themselves to entertaining and gift giving. She builds recipes that are well written and easy to duplicate. Yvette provides the reader with gift labels, packaging sources, and serving suggestion cards. From an Herb Marinated Feta recipe she provides the foundation for one of my favorites, Feta Palmiers. Quick, easy and delicious party delectable delights that are perfect for entertaining and gifting.

It should be obvious by now that I will be clearing a space on my bookshelf for the first in her series of books. I'm sure that they will provide many hours of creative fun, producing results that can be gifted to family, friends, and strangers alike.

What better way to expand your circle of influence? Read this book, cook with joy and pay it forward!!

Introduction

Mrs. Irma Ramos' glitter cookies began my obsession with edible gifts. As a young child, my family would receive these red and green glittery treats every Christmas season. By the time I was 12 years old I was making batch after batch and sharing them with neighbors and friends. I've been giving edible gifts for as long as I can remember. The majority of my gift giving occurs during the Thanksgiving/Christmas season, but it has grown into a year-round affair. I love it when family and friends call to remind me about their birthday, and they drop hints as to which edible gift they'd like to receive. This cookbook is inspired by those requests that I've enjoyed making throughout the years.

Each year as the holidays arrive, my freezer and refrigerator quickly fill up with edible gifts to share. I've discovered that having edible gifts on hand allowed for easy entertaining during the holidays. My passion for casual entertaining has led me to transform these edible gifts into easy-to-prepare dishes. I simply incorporate an edible gift from my stash into whatever I need at the time whether it be a breakfast item or an afternoon appetizer.

I've also discovered that edible gifts are a much appreciated hostess gift. Throughout the year, but especially when the holiday season is upon us, we attend parties and gather at the home of family and friends. Homemade gifts are a lovely way to show your host how much you appreciate them. When attending dinner parties, it is important to know you host. This is not always possible, but with just a little foresight you can create a hostess gift that will leave you with an invitation to return. If you would like to provide a gift to be enjoyed during the dinner party, make it easy for your host to set up by bringing it as prepared as possible. Perhaps a jar of pistachio thyme dip (page 31) and a fresh baguette that will be a welcomed gift during cocktail hour, but it won't steal the show. If you know that your host likes to stick to the set menu, then consider bringing something they'll enjoy the following day. Perhaps something for tomorrows breakfast such as Bacon Jam Quiche (page 56), biscotti (page 80) or scones (pages 90, 93). These are a nice surprise when staying at someone's home, and they give your host a break from cooking. Everyone will enjoy your breakfast-time treat while sipping coffee around the kitchen table. Edible gifts are always a much appreciated treat, and truly capture the seasons spirit of sharing.

How to Use This Book

This book is organized by one edible gift chapter at a time. Each chapter also includes recipes that transform that edible gift into other dishes. You'll also find packaging ideas to inspire your gift wrapping and basket bundling of these recipes. Take a peek at My Favorite Things section (pg 12) for a lists of websites that have every type of jar, twine, tissue and accessories for packaging your edible gifts. At the end of each chapter there are templates for gift tags, serving suggestion tags and baking instruction cards that can easily be scanned or photocopied. Simply cut out and attach the tags with ribbon or twine when sharing these delicious gifts. Everyone loves receiving a gift in the mail. If your plans include shipping an edible gift, I have listed my packaging and mailing tips (pg 11) to ensure the safe arrival of your gift.

Having a stash of edible gifts has been a timesaver during the busiest weeks of the year when I'm hosting houseguest, and attending family gatherings and parties. If you set aside some time to create a few of these recipes, you'll find them incredibly convenient when you're in need of a breakfast item, a quick appetizer or simply a last minute gift.

Shipping Edible Gifts…
and tips to ensure their safe arrival

The best edible gifts for mailing are non-refrigerated items that are safe to consume at room temperature, and those that stay fresher longer. Moist and firm baked goods, rather than brittle and delicate treats ship well and arrive in the best form.

I prefer to send non-refrigerated edible gifts to avoid the use of gel-paks, dry ice and the potential for perished gifts.

Bake your edible gift as close to shipping time as possible. Factor in cooling time, set time, drying time. I usually prepare edible gifts the night before, and allow an overnight cooling time.

Don't wrap and send edible gifts that haven't cooled completely. The steam will create condensation making for a soggy gift.

Cake boards are your friend with dense and dry baked goods. Place firm baked goods such as the Strawberry Poppy Seed cake, biscotti, scones, or cookies on a cake board. Seal tightly with plastic wrap to secure in place.

Another packaging tip to keep cookies from breaking is to create a cushion with crumpled wax paper or parchment on the bottom of a re-sealable container or tin. Place cookies in single layers with crumpled wax paper or parchment in between layers.

Snuggly top with a layer of crumpled wax paper or parchment and seal with lid.

Protect jars and bottles with a 2-inch cushion of bubble wrap. Then place each bottle in a re-sealable bag just in case it leaks or is crushed.

Pack edible gifts as snuggly as possible in a sturdy box. Provide enough cushion, about 2 inches around all items, and pack with foam peanuts, bubble wrap, Instapak or tightly crumpled paper.

Include a note on the best way to serve and store the edible gift once it arrives.

Use packaging tape to best seal the box, and to withstand the bumpy ride ahead. Although it's adorable, don't wrap your box in brown paper or tie with string. This can get caught in sorting belts.

Ship your gift earlier in the week so your package doesn't sit in a warehouse over the weekend.

Whenever possible, send edible gifts with a fast shipping time. Let the recipient know when to expect your treat so that it doesn't sit in the cold or heat all day, but most importantly so they can enjoy it as soon as possible!

A Few Of My Favorite Things…
and where to find them

I find it helpful to have a shelf or large drawer stocked with supplies for packaging edible gifts. You can purchase an array of supplies online such as bottles, jars, ribbons, twine, cake boxes and cellophane bags. I've listed my favorite sites where I purchase the bottles, jars, ribbons and packaging supplies used throughout this book.

BOTTLES & JARS

bormioliroccousa.com	potterybarn.com
freshpreserving.com	surlatable.com
heb.com	uline.com
hobbylobby.com	weckjars.com
leparfait.com	williams-sonoma.com
michaels.com	worldmarket.com

CANDY BOXES, CAKE BOXES & CAKE BOARDS

brpboxshop.com

clearbags.com

hobbylobby.com

michaels.com

nashvillewraps.com

BUTCHER PAPER, KRAFT PAPER & DECORATIVE TAPE

cutetape.com

hobbylobby.com

michaels.com

papersource.com

pospaper.com

shopangelaliguori.com

uline.com

CELLOPHANE, BURLAP, MUSLIN, GLASSINE & PAPER BAGS

brpboxshop.com

clearbags.com

hobbylobby.com

michaels.com

nashvillewraps.com

shopangelaliguori.com

RIBBONS & TWINE

abchome.com

clearbags.com

hobbylobby.com

michaels.com

nashvillewraps.com

papersource.com

shopangelaliguori.com

PRINTING PAPER

officedepot.com

papersource.com

staples.com

SHIPPING BOXES & PACKAGING SUPPLIES

nashvillewraps.com

officedepot.com

staples.com

uline.com

1. Herb Marinated Feta

This flavorful recipe, which has a beautiful presentation, requires minimal preparation time. The blend of herbs, spices and feta cheese are delightful. For easy entertaining spoon marinated feta onto crusty bread and served with a bottle of wine. Easily transform the marinated feta into flaky palmiers or layer into a grape and feta tart. Be sure to use leftover olive oil for flavorful dressings and marinades.

1 lb. feta cheese block, cut
    into bite-size cubes
2 teaspoons dried oregano
1 teaspoon dried thyme
    leaves
1/2 teaspoon crushed red
    pepper flakes
1/2 teaspoon fresh
cracked black pepper

rosemary sprigs, thyme
    sprigs, or bay leaves for
    garnishing

about 1 cup olive oil, enough
    to cover feta in each jar

Special equipment: Three
    8-ounce jars with
    resealable lids

Herb Marinated Feta

You won't believe how quickly you can prepare this herb marinated feta. You'll also enjoy discovering the endless ways you can serve the salty chunks of herb infused cheese.

1. In a large mixing bowl, gently toss the feta cheese, oregano, thyme, red pepper, and black pepper until the cheese is evenly coated.
2. Arrange the coated cheese in the three jars. Decoratively place springs of herbs or leaves inside each jar. Fill jars with enough olive oil to cover the cheese. Seal jars with lids and refrigerate for 8 hours and up to 2 weeks.
Serve chilled or room temperature.

Serving suggestion tag and gift tags for this recipe on page 24.

Serving Suggestions:

- Spoon marinated feta onto crackers or toast for an easy appetizer.
- Include feta crumbles in your salads and on your cheese platters.
- Toss with sundried tomatoes and fill endive leaves for an appetizer.
- Toss with tomatoes and chickpeas then stuff in a pita for your office lunch.
- Toss with roasted vegetable to enhance the flavor.
- Make dinner in minutes by tossing the herbed cheese and the flavored oil with pasta.
- Use the leftover oil for marinades and vinaigrettes.

This no-fuss, no-cooking required recipe is truly a beautiful treat, and a much appreciated gift.

If you can unfold a sheet of puff pastry and crumble feta, you have all the necessary skills to make this delectable treat. You'll love them as an appetizer or piled onto a cheese board.

Feta Palmiers

Savory palmiers are an easy and elegant treat made with nothing more than ready made puff pastry, herb marinated feta and a sprinkle of salt. The flavorful feta combined with the crunch of the pastry will have you making batch after batch. They're a great accompaniment to a cheese platter, and make beautifully packaged hostess gifts.

1. Heat oven to 400°F. Line a rimmed baking sheet with parchment.
2. On a floured surface, roll puff pastry to a 9x15 rectangle. Transfer to prepared baking sheet.
3. Use a fork to remove feta from jar, draining off oil. Arrange feta on top of puff pastry. Working from one of the long sides, tightly roll puff pastry until you reach the middle. Repeat with the other side until the rolled edges touch in the middle. Transfer to prepared baking sheet and freeze until firm, 30-45 minutes.
4. Cut the rolled pastry into 1/2-inch slices and arrange slices on parchment at least 1-inch apart. Brush with oil from the jar of marinated feta and sprinkle with salt. Bake in the preheated oven until golden and crisp, about 30 minutes. Let cool completely on baking sheets.

Gift tags for this recipe on page 24.

Do Ahead: Filled rolls of puff pastry can be wrapped in plastic wrap, placed in a resealable freezer bag and stored in the freezer up to 1 week. Slice frozen rolls, brush with oil, sprinkle with salt then bake as directed. Palmiers can be baked up to 8 hours ahead and stored at room temperature.

SERVINGS: 30 palmiers

1 8-ounce jar herbed marinated feta
1 sheet 8-ounce frozen puff pastry, thawed
kosher salt

Flour for dusting rolling
　　surface
1 8-ounce sheet frozen puff
　　pastry, thawed
1 8-ounce jar, herbed
　　marinated feta, (about
　　2/3 cup feta), reserve oil
1/2 cup red seedless grapes,
　　cut in half
2-3 Tablespoons balsamic
　　vinegar reduction glaze

Roasted Grape & Feta Tart

Head straight to your kitchen and whip up sweet and savory flavors that sit on a bed of flaky puff pastry. You'll enjoy preparing this beautiful appetizer which is perfect for a fête during any season.

1. Preheat oven to 400°F. Line a baking sheet with parchment.
2. On a floured surface, roll pastry into a 12x9-inch rectangle. Use water to moisten a 1/2-inch border on all four sides. Fold the moistened edges inward. Use the tines of a fork to press and seal the edge on all four sides. Pierce center of pastry all over with fork. Transfer pastry to prepared baking sheet and place in freezer until firm, 15-20 minutes.
3. With the tip of a sharp knife, lightly score a border just inside the folded edge. Lightly brush the edges with the reserved oil, and bake until puffed and golden brown, 10-12 minutes.
4. Crumble marinated feta onto the baked pastry. Top feta with grapes, cut side down. Bake until feta and grapes are warm, and the edges are deep golden brown, 15-20 minutes.
5. Transfer to a wire rack to cool for 5 minutes. Drizzle to taste with balsamic glaze. Cut and serve warm or room temperature.

Gift tags for this recipe on page 24.

Sweet grapes, tart feta, and tangy balsamic glaze blend into a crowd pleasing recipe that pairs beautifully with a glass of wine. Add a leafy green salad to this appetizer and it can double as a light dinner.

HERB MARINATED FETA

Serving Suggestions

- SPOON ONTO BAGUETTE SLICES OR
  ENDIVE LEAVES FOR APPETIZERS
- ADD IN SALADS OR ON CHEESE BOARDS
- STUFF PITA WITH FETA, TOMATO, AND CHICKPEAS
- TOSS FETA AND OIL WITH PASTA
- USE LEFTOVER OIL FOR VINAIGRETTES

A YDELICACIES.COM RECIPE

The simple components of oil, cheese, spices and herbs create a lovely no-cook gift. The jars can be tucked into a basket full of complimentary items such as a baguette, fruit, and a bottle of wine. The tasty jars are just as special given on their own with a serving suggestion tag. I always make extra for myself to enhance any dish, or to simply eat straight from the jar.

HERB MARINATED FETA

Serving Suggestions

- SPOON ONTO BAGUETTE SLICES OR
  ENDIVE LEAVES FOR APPETIZERS
- ADD IN SALADS OR ON CHEESE BOARDS
- STUFF PITA WITH FETA, TOMATO,
  AND CHICKPEAS
- TOSS FETA AND OIL WITH PASTA
- USE LEFTOVER OIL FOR VINAIGRETTES

A YDELICACIES.COM RECIPE

HERB MARINATED FETA

Serving Suggestions

- SPOON ONTO BAGUETTE SLICES OR
  ENDIVE LEAVES FOR APPETIZERS
- ADD IN SALADS OR ON CHEESE BOARDS
- STUFF PITA WITH FETA, TOMATO,
  AND CHICKPEAS
- TOSS FETA AND OIL WITH PASTA
- USE LEFTOVER OIL FOR VINAIGRETTES

A YDELICACIES.COM RECIPE

TAG INSTRUCTIONS

1. Photocopy or scan tags onto cardstock. Alternately, go to **Ydelicacies.com** and search **"printables"**.

2. Open scanned/photocopied file or website file and print tags onto cardstock.

3. Use scissors or craft knife to cut out tags.

4. Fold and crease Herb Marinated Feta Serving Suggestion tags. Punch out hole through both thicknesses of card stock with a hole punch. For Feta Palmier and Roasted Grape & Feta Tart tags punch out hole in single thickness of card stock.

5. String decorative ribbon or twine through the hole and tie tag to edible gift.

2. Pistachio Honey

Vibrant green pistachios, and the bright flavor of orange zest delicately pair with honey for a versatile condiment. It's amazingly delicious served with cheese, and quite elegant drizzled on a pear and ricotta tart. This no-cook condiment can be swirled into oatmeal or ice cream for added flavor or folded into sour cream for an easy dip.

SERVINGS: five 6-ounce jars

2 cups shelled pistachios,
    coarsely chopped
3 Tablespoons orange zest
3 cups honey
special equipment:
five 6-ounce jars with
    resealable lids

Pistachio Honey

Honey gets a delicious infusion with the addition of orange zest and pistachios. This little condiment is so easy to prepare it will become your go-to no-cook edible gift.

1. In a medium bowl, stir the pistachios and orange zest together until combined.
2. Add honey and stir until well combined. Pour into jars, seal with lids and refrigerate up to 4 weeks.

Serving suggestion tag and gift tags for this recipe on page 36.

Serving Suggestions:
- Stir into yogurt and berries for an easy morning meal
- Drizzle on goat cheese for a quick and tasty dip
- Toss with roasted carrots for a flavorful side dish
- Drizzle on sliced pears and serve on Brie wedges for party food bites
- Serve on pound cake and top with whipped cream for dessert

Sweet, crunchy and bursting with flavor these beautiful jars are perfect for holiday gifting.

Scoop this dip into decorative jars, and create a hostess gift that is easily packaged with veggies, a baguette or your favorite crackers.

Pistachio Thyme Dip

If you're in need of a snack or appetize this must-make dip can be prepared in minutes. Pistachio, thyme and tangy sour cream blend into a flavorful dip. Shhh, don't tell anyone, but there's goat cheese, too. I've had more people tell me, after tasting this dip, that this is the first time they've enjoyed goat cheese.

1. In a medium bowl, blend the goat cheese, sour cream, olive oil and honey together until smooth.
2. Add the thyme leaves, lemon zest, salt and pepper and stir until well combined. Refrigerate until ready to serve. Garnish with a drizzle of pistachio honey before serving.

Gift tags for this recipe on page 36.

Gift tags for this recipe on page 36.

SERVINGS: 6-8

8 oz. goat cheese
1/3 cup sour cream
1 Tablespoon olive oil
1 teaspoon pistachio honey, plus extra for garnish
2 teaspoons fresh thyme leaves
1 teaspoon lemon zest
1/4 teaspoon kosher salt
1/4 teaspoon fresh cracked pepper

PASTRY

1 sheet 8 ounce frozen
puff pastry, thawed
1 egg, beaten

TOPPINGS

3 large Bosc pears,
(1 1/4 lbs.) cored and thinly
    sliced
1 Tablespoon olive oil
1/4 teaspoon black pepper
1 cup ricotta
1/4 teaspoon kosher salt
2 Tablespoons pistachio
    honey, plus more for
    garnish

Pear & Ricotta Tart

This tasty appetizer will easily transform into a light dinner when garnished with fresh cracked pepper and served with a salad. Surprisingly, this mildly sweet and creamy tart is also a dessert favorite when garnished with a generous drizzle of pistachio honey.

PASTRY

1. Heat oven to 400°F. Line a rimmed baking sheet with parchment.
2. On a floured surface, roll puff pastry into a 12X10-inch rectangle. Cut into 3 strips that are 4X10-inches each. Transfer to the prepared baking sheet and freeze for 15 minutes.
3. With the tip of a knife, lightly score a quarter inch border around each frozen pastry strip. Brush with egg wash and bake until the center is puffed and golden brown, 10-12 minutes.

TOPPINGS

1. In a medium bowl gently toss sliced pears with olive oil and black pepper. Set aside.
2. In a small bowl, stir ricotta, salt, and honey together. Divide and spread within the borders of the three baked pastries.
3. Decoratively top with the sliced pears. Bake in the preheated oven until the edges of the pastry are deep golden brown and the pears are lightly softened, 20-25 minutes.
4. Drizzle with pistachio honey and serve warm or room temperature.

DO AHEAD: The puff pastry strips can be baked 4 hours ahead and set aside until ready to add toppings. The tarts can be baked 2 hour ahead and stored at room temperature. If serving warm, reheat in a 350°F oven for 8-10 minutes before serving.

Gift tags for this recipe on page 36.

This delicious tart will look like you spent hours in the kitchen. Serve as an afternoon snack or add this entertaining favorite to your party menu.

You can easily create a thoughtful hostess gift by tucking a jar of pistachio honey in a basket with a selection of cheeses, crusty bread and a bottle of wine. Gift giving doesn't get any easier than this, zero cooking required.

The lightest drizzle of pistachio honey compliments the salty nature of cheese. It's delicious combined with Parmigiano-Reggiano and Manchego, yet lovely with soft, creamy cheese as well. Uncork a bottle of dry white wine, slice crusty bread and in a matter of minutes your party host will be ready to serve a crowd.

PEAR & RICOTTA

TART

A YDELICACIES.COM RECIPE

PEAR & RICOTTA

TART

A YDELICACIES.COM RECIPE

PEAR & RICOTTA

TART

A YDELICACIES.COM RECIPE

PISTACHIO THYME

DIP

A YDELICACIES.COM RECIPE

PISTACHIO THYME

DIP

A YDELICACIES.COM RECIPE

PISTACHIO THYME

DIP

A YDELICACIES.COM RECIPE

PISTACHIO HONEY

Serving Suggestions

- STIR INTO YOGURT AND BERRIES
FOR BREAKFAST
- DRIZZLE ON GOAT CHEESE FOR
AN EASY DIP
- TOSS WITH ROASTED CARROTS FOR
AN EASY SIDE DISH
- SERVE WITH POUND CAKE AND
WHIPPED CREAM

A YDELICACIES.COM RECIPE

PISTACHIO HONEY

Serving Suggestions

- STIR INTO YOGURT AND BERRIES
FOR BREAKFAST
- DRIZZLE ON GOAT CHEESE FOR
AN EASY DIP
- TOSS WITH ROASTED CARROTS FOR
AN EASY SIDE DISH
- SERVE WITH POUND CAKE AND
WHIPPED CREAM

A YDELICACIES.COM RECIPE

TAG INSTRUCTIONS

1. Photocopy or scan tags onto cardstock. Alternately, go to **Ydelicacies.com** and search **"printables"**.

2. Open scanned/photo-copied file or website file and print tags onto cardstock.

3. Use scissors or craft knife to cut out tags.

4. Fold and crease Pistachio Honey Serving Suggestion tags. Punch out hole through both thicknesses of card stock with a hole punch. For Pear & Ricotta Tart and Pistachio Thyme Dip tags punch out hole in single thickness of card stock.

5. String decorative ribbon or twine through the hole and tie tag to edible gift.

3. Strawberry Jam

When there's homemade jam in my refrigerator it gains a new life with both sweet and savory dishes. Layer jam into cake batter for a sweet surprise such as my Strawberry Poppy Seed Cake. For a dreamy dessert, drizzle strawberry jam on cloudlike meringues, which are always a dessert favorite. For a savory twist, whisk a spoonful into vinaigrette to balance acidity. Stir redpepper flakes into jam, and brush onto chicken or ribs for a deliciously sticky glaze. From desserts to glazes, strawberry jam is the perfect add-in to just about anything.

Strawberry Jam

SERVINGS: 2 cups

2 lbs. strawberries, stems
    removed
1 cup sugar
1 Tablespoon lemon juice
two 8-ounce jars with lids

This small batch jam is delicious and easy to prepare. Who knew that jam doesn't have to go through the canning process? It will keep for up to a month in the refrigerator when stored in airtight containers, making this an excellent gift. You might make this recipe for gifting, but be prepared to keep a jar for yourself.

1. Crush each strawberry with your hands until almost falling apart.
2. Place crushed strawberries and any released juices, sugar and lemon juice into a medium heavy pot. Bring to a boil, frequently stirring, until sugar is dissolved and more juices are released, 3-5 minutes.
3. Reduce to a simmer, stirring occasionally, and cook until the juices reduce to a jam like consistency, 30-40 minutes.
4. Divide between jars, cover and chill. Store in the refrigerator up to 1 month.

Serving suggestion tag and gift tags for this recipe on page 48.

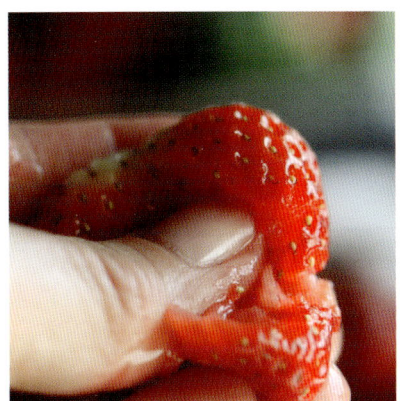

Making jam doesn't have to be intimidating. My recipe is easy to prepare, and doesn't require processing the jars for long-term storage. Simply store the jars in your refrigerator. Trust me, it won't last long.

This delicious strawberry jam filled cake is quite elegant simply served with a dusting of powdered sugar.

Strawberry Poppy Seed Cake

Baking this cake means there's no worries about splitting cake layers and frosting to make. Strawberry jam is baked right into the cake which allows you to simply serve with a dusting of powdered sugar. Your favorite strawberry jam will suffice, but if you're in the midst of strawberry season try my strawberry jam recipe. The flavor combination of nutty poppy seeds, crunchy almonds and sweet jam make this an irresistible cake. The texture is deliciously dense, making it sturdy enough to be packaged and mailed cross country, for a treat that will delight your recipient.

1. Preheat oven to 325°F. For easy removal of the cake, place a 4-inch wide strip of parchment that sits on the bottom, up the sides and overlaps the edges of a 8x3-inch round pan. Line the bottom of the pan with parchment. Grease and flour the sides and the parchment.

2. In a large mixing bowl, beat the sugar and butter until combined into a pebbly texture. Add the eggs and almond extract and beat until light and creamy, 2-3 minutes. Add the flour, poppy seeds and salt and mix until combined.

3. Evenly spread half the batter into the prepared pan. Spread the jam on top of the batter leaving a 1-inch border of batter. Drop spoonfuls of the remaining batter on top, and evenly smooth the batter. Sprinkle the almonds on top, and bake until a cake tester inserted into the center comes out clean, about 90 minutes. Cool completely before removing from pan. Dust the top with powdered sugar and serve.

Gift tags for this recipe on page 48.

SERVINGS: 10-12

2 cups granulated sugar
1 cup butter, softened
4 large eggs
2 teaspoons almond extract
2 cups all-purpose flour
2 Tablespoon poppy seeds
1 teaspoon kosher salt
2/3 cup strawberry jam
2/3 cup sliced almonds
1 Tablespoon powdered
    sugar

6 egg whites

2 teaspoons cornstarch

1/8 teaspoon kosher salt

1 cup granulated sugar

1 cup powdered sugar

2 Tablespoons unsweetened
    cocoa powder

2 ounces dark chocolate,
    chopped into thin chips

1/2 cup strawberry jam

Chocolate Chunk Meringues with a Strawberry Drizzle

Whip up some egg whites and swirl in some chocolate for meringues that will make a big statement on your dessert table. These little creations can be enjoyed with a drizzle of jam, and are gorgeous when packaged for gifting.

1. Preheat oven to 275°F. Line a baking sheet with parchment.
2. In a large bowl, whisk the egg whites, cornstarch and salt on medium speed until frothy, 1-2 minutes.
3. While beating the egg whites, slowly add the granulated sugar and beat on medium-high speed until soft peaks form, 5-7 minutes. Slowly add the powdered sugar and beat on high speed until glossy and stiff peaks form, about 5 minutes.
4. Fold the cocoa powder and chocolate into the egg whites to create chocolate streaks.
5. Using a large spoon, mound 12 meringues on the prepared baking sheet. Bake until dry and firm, about 1 1/2 hours. Serve with a drizzle of strawberry jam.

Gift tags for this recipe on page 48.

If you enjoy crisp, billowy creations with a burst of chocolate and strawberry, this is a dessert you must try.

Homemade gifts best capture the seasons spirit of sharing. An added plus is no worries about sizes or colors to exchange. I enjoy preparing a few recipes and dividing the batches among gift boxes. The recipes in this chapter were divided and placed into hat style boxes. These make great gifts for the office or an entire family to enjoy during the hustle and bustle of the holiday season.

STRAWBERRY
POPPY SEED

CAKE

A YDELICACIES.COM RECIPE

STRAWBERRY
POPPY SEED

CAKE

A YDELICACIES.COM RECIPE

STRAWBERRY
POPPY SEED

CAKE

A YDELICACIES.COM RECIPE

CHOCOLATE
CHUNK

MERINGUES

A YDELICACIES.COM RECIPE

CHOCOLATE
CHUNK

MERINGUES

A YDELICACIES.COM RECIPE

CHOCOLATE
CHUNK

MERINGUES

A YDELICACIES.COM RECIPE

TAG INSTRUCTIONS

1. Photocopy or scan tags onto cardstock. Alternately, go to **Ydelicacies.com** and search **"printables"**.

2. Open scanned/photo-copied file or website file and print tags onto cardstock.

3. Use scissors or craft knife to cut out tags.

4. Fold and crease Strawberry Jam Serving Suggestion tags. Punch out hole through both thicknesses of card stock with a hole punch. For Strawberry Poppy Seed Cake and Chocolate Chunk Meringues tags punch out hole in single thickness of card stock.

5. String decorative ribbon or twine through the hole and tie tag to edible gift.

STRAWBERRY JAM

Serving Suggestions

- DRIZZLE ON A SUNDAE
- SPREAD ON TOAST OR BISCUITS
- SWIRL INTO YOGURT OR OATMEAL
- TOP A CHEESE CAKE
- DOLLOP ON PANCAKES OR WAFFLES
- FILL A LAYER CAKE

A YDELICACIES.COM RECIPE

STRAWBERRY JAM

Serving Suggestions

- DRIZZLE ON A SUNDAE
- SPREAD ON TOAST OR BISCUITS
- SWIRL INTO YOGURT OR OATMEAL
- TOP A CHEESE CAKE
- DOLLOP ON PANCAKES OR WAFFLES
- FILL A LAYER CAKE

A YDELICACIES.COM RECIPE

4. Bacon Jam

Bacon jam is a versatile condiment that will add a pop of flavor to any dish. The blend of sweet and savory is a great addition to your entertaining menu and for gift giving, too. It adds an unexpected layer of flavor to quiche, and the perfect amount of tanginess to a vinaigrette. If you serve this during your holiday entertaining, be sure to make an extra batch to send home with your guest. They'll thank you.

Bacon Jam

This versatile condiment is perfect for spreading on toast, layering in a burger or in a grilled cheese sandwich. It adds the perfect amount of tanginess to a vinaigrette and is fantastic swirled into a quiche. Keep this on hand during the holidays season as a condiment for your entertaining menu or for an ideal edible gift.

SERVINGS: 2 cups

1 lb. sliced bacon
2 Tablespoons bacon drippings
4 cups yellow onions, diced
1/2 cup brewed coffee
3/4 cup balsamic vinegar
1/2 cup maple syrup
1 1/2 cups dark brown sugar, packed
2 Tablespoons fresh garlic, minced
2 teaspoons chili powder
2 teaspoons dry ground mustard
1 1/2 teaspoons dried thyme leaves
1/2 teaspoon fresh cracked black pepper

1. In a large skillet on medium heat, place bacon slices in a single layer and cook in batches until bacon is crisp and fat is rendered. Transfer bacon to paper towels to cool. When cool enough to handle, finely chop bacon and set aside. Pour rendered fat into a strainer placed over a bowl. Reserve fat and clean the skillet.
2. Return skillet to medium heat. Add 2 Tablespoons of reserved bacon fat and onions. Cook until onions are translucent, 8-10 minutes.
3. Add coffee, vinegar, syrup, brown sugar, garlic, chili powder, mustard, thyme and black pepper. Bring to a boil and let boil for 2 minutes, stirring frequently.
4. Add chopped bacon and reduce to a simmer. Simmer, stirring occasionally, until the liquid reduces to a syrup like consistency, 50-60 minutes. Pour into airtight containers, and store in the refrigerator up to 4 weeks.

Serving suggestion tag and gift tags for this recipe on page 62.

If you're entertaining calls for a quick and easy appetizer, spread burrata or brie on crostini, and top with bacon jam for a delightful treat.

53

Easily elegant when arranged on a serving platter, and the perfect party nibble when you're holding a glass.

54

Bacon Jam & Mushroom Hand Salad

This forkless salad is bursting with crunch and packed with flavor. I often serve these flavorful appetizers with Romaine leaves, but Bibb lettuce or Little Gem lettuce works beautifully, too.

1. Arrange lettuce leaves on serving platter and refrigerate.
2. In a medium skillet over medium heat, sauté mushrooms with 1 Tablespoon olive oil until tender, 4-6 minutes. Remove pan from heat.
3. In a small bowl whisk together bacon jam, remaining Tablespoon of olive oil, and rice vinegar until emulsified. Stir into mushrooms until well combined.
4. Using a small spoon, divide the mushroom filling among the lettuce leaves. Garnish with chives and serve immediately.

SERVINGS: 4

6 oz. Romaine leaves
2 Tablespoons olive oil, divided
8 oz. sliced mushrooms
2 Tablespoons bacon jam
1 teaspoon rice vinegar
1 Tablespoons chives, chopped

SERVINGS: 8

1 1/4 cups all-purpose flour,
    plus more for work surface
1/2 teaspoon kosher salt
1/2 cup (1 stick) frozen,
    unsalted butter
1/4 cup ice water
1 1/2 teaspoons white or
    apple cider vinegar

FILLING

6 eggs
1/2 cup heavy whipping
    cream
1/4 cup bacon jam, plus
extra for spreading on top
8 oz. Gruyere cheese
(about 2 cups), grated

Bacon Jam Quiche

You'll enjoy this quiche which is packed with flavor from Gruyere cheese and bacon jam. House guest will enjoy the blend of flavors all inside a golden, flaky pastry crust.

PASTRY CRUST

1. Preheat oven to 425°F.
2. In a medium bowl, whisk flour and salt together. Grate butter into the bowl, and toss to coat with the flour.
3. Stir ice water and vinegar together, and sprinkle over the flour/butter mixture. Using your hands, combine the mixture until it comes together in pebble size pieces. Some of the flour will not be incorporated. Using your hands, rub while flattening the butter and the loose flour between your fingertips. Continue this motion until all the flour is incorporated. If necessary, add 1 teaspoon of water to incorporate the flour.
4. Gather the dough together. Dust the rolling surface with flour, and roll the dough to a 12- inch round.
5. Gently wrap the dough around the rolling pin, and transfer to the pie dish. Unroll and place the dough over hanging the dish.
6. Gently fit the crust into the pie dish. Decoratively crimp the edge. Freeze the crust until firm, about 20 minutes.
7. Line the crust with parchment leaving a generous overhang and fill with pie weights or dried beans. Bake until the crust is golden brown around the edges, about 15 minutes.
8. Remove the parchment and beans, and return the shell to the oven until the bottom of the crust is dry and set, 10-15 minutes.

FILLING

1. Reduce oven temperature to 350°F.
2. In a medium bowl, whisk together the eggs, heavy whipping cream and bacon jam until combined.
3. Fold in the cheese and pour into the prepared crust. Bake until the filling is set, 40-45 minutes. Spread a thin layer of bacon jam on top. Let cool at least 10 minutes before cutting.

Gift tags for this recipe on page 62.

A great quiche is all about a homemade crust, however, I occasionally use store bought crust when my time is limited. You'll discover that this filling is so delicious, it will yield impressive results with either crust.

Caramelized pears, bacon jam and arugula are a perfect combination for an autumn inspired salad!

Pear Salad with Bacon Jam Vinaigrette

Create an incredible salad with tangy bacon jam vinaigrette and caramelized pears. Beautifully presented on a bed of arugula it's a must-have on your holiday table. The vinaigrette is a tasty gift that can be tossed in quinoa salads, drizzled on roasted asparagus or on grilled fish.

VINAIGRETTE

1. In a microwave safe dish warm the jam, 5-10 seconds.
2. Whisk in the olive oil and rice vinegar until emulsified. Vinaigrette can be prepared 1 hour ahead and set aside at room temperature.

WALNUTS & PEARS

1. In a dry medium skillet over medium heat, cook the walnuts until toasted, 2-4 minutes. Transfer to a plate or a paper towel until ready to assemble salad.
2. Cut pears in half, core and remove seeds. Cut each half into 3 wedges.
3. Heat olive oil in a medium skillet over medium heat. Working in batches, arrange the pear wedges in a single layer with cut side down. Cook until lightly brown, 2-3 minutes. Flip to the other cut side and cook until lightly brown. Transfer to a cooling rack set over parchment or a baking sheet to catch the drips. Let sit until ready to assemble salad, up to 1 hour.

ASSEMBLY

1. In a medium bowl, toss arugula with 1/4 cup bacon jam vinaigrette.
2. Arrange arugula on a serving platter. Top with caramelized pears and toasted walnuts.
   Drizzle 1 Tablespoon bacon jam vinaigrette on pears, and serve immediately.

Serving suggestion tag and gift tags for this recipe on page 62.

SERVINGS: 4-6

BACON JAM VINAIGRETTE
Makes 1/2 cup vinaigrette
1/4 cup bacon jam
3 Tablespoons olive oil
2 Tablespoons rice vinegar

WALNUTS & PEARS
1 teaspoon olive oil
2 Bosc pears, (about 1 lb.) refrigerated
1 cup walnuts, chopped
5 oz. arugula

BACON JAM

Serving Suggestions

· SPREAD ON TOAST OR CRACKERS
· FOLD INTO AN OMELET
· WHISK INTO A VINAIGRETTE
· STIR INTO SOUR CREAM FOR AN EASY DIP
· LAYER IN A BURGER OR GRILLED
CHEESE SANDWICH

AYDELICACIES.COM RECIPE

When you transform bacon into this sweet and savory jam or the vinaigrette, be prepared to share. Simply create a gift by packing bacon jam in glass jars or ceramic ramekins paired with cheddar cheese and a baguette. If you're in need of a hostess gift, package bacon jam vinaigrette in glass bottles, and bundle in a basket with toasted walnuts and seasonal pears. Everyone will enjoy this unexpected flavor combination tossed with salad greens.

BACON JAM — VINAIGRETTE — A YDELICACIES.COM RECIPE

BACON JAM — VINAIGRETTE — A YDELICACIES.COM RECIPE

BACON JAM — VINAIGRETTE — A YDELICACIES.COM RECIPE

BACON JAM — QUICHE — A YDELICACIES.COM RECIPE

BACON JAM — QUICHE — A YDELICACIES.COM RECIPE

BACON JAM — QUICHE — A YDELICACIES.COM RECIPE

BACON JAM

Serving Suggestions

- SPREAD ON TOAST OR CRACKERS
- FOLD INTO AN OMELET
- WHISK INTO A VINAIGRETTE
- STIR INTO SOUR CREAM FOR AN EASY DIP
- LAYER IN A BURGER OR GRILLED
  CHEESE SANDWICH

A YDELICACIES.COM RECIPE

BACON JAM

Serving Suggestions

- SPREAD ON TOAST OR CRACKERS
- FOLD INTO AN OMELET
- WHISK INTO A VINAIGRETTE
- STIR INTO SOUR CREAM FOR AN EASY DIP
- LAYER IN A BURGER OR GRILLED
  CHEESE SANDWICH

A YDELICACIES.COM RECIPE

TAG INSTRUCTIONS

1. Photocopy or scan tags onto cardstock. Alternately, go to **Ydelicacies.com** and search **"printables"**.

2. Open scanned/photo-copied file or website file and print tags onto cardstock.

3. Use scissors or craft knife to cut out tags.

4. Fold and crease Bacon Jam Serving Suggestion tags. Punch out hole through both thicknesses of card stock with a hole punch. For Bacon Jam Quiche and Bacon Jam Vinaigrette tags punch out hole in single thickness of card stock.

5. String decorative ribbon or twine through the hole and tie tag to edible gift.

5. Candied Thyme Pecans

Candied pecans are a favorite snack during the holidays, and easy to make from ingredients you probably have on hand. The combination of savory and sweet with a touch of heat are perfect to bring to any party. If your holidays include travel plans, these are easy to pack as a travel snack, too.

For added flavor, try mixing them into chicken salad or toss with roasted squash for a sweet surprise. Create a tasty cheese board by coating goat cheese with chopped candied pecans or simply add them as an accompaniment. There is nothing easier to make that pleases a crowd than candied thyme pecans.

Candied Thyme Pecans

SERVINGS: 5 cups

1/2 cup brown sugar, packed
1/3 cup granulated sugar
1 Tablespoon dried thyme
1 teaspoon kosher salt
1/4 teaspoon cayenne
    pepper
3 cups (12 ounces)
pecans halves, unsalted
1 egg white

Candied thyme pecans combine a touch of sweetness with savory spices for a holiday treat you will make more than once. This simple recipe is one I use not only for holidays, but throughout the year. These pecans are fabulous in a salad, with roasted acorn squash, folded into a grain salad, or as a game day/tailgating munchie.

1. Preheat oven to 300°F. Line a rimmed baking sheet with parchment or a silicone mat.
2. In a small bowl, whisk together the brown sugar, granulated sugar, thyme, salt and cayenne pepper until well combined. Set aside.
3. In a medium bowl, whisk the egg white until frothy. Add pecans and toss until evenly coated. Add the sugar mixture, and toss until pecans are well coated.
4. Arrange coated pecans in a single layer on the prepared baking sheet. Bake in the preheated oven for 20 minutes.
5. Remove baking sheet from the oven and stir the pecans.
6. Return baking sheet to the oven, and continue baking until the pecans are fragrant and the coating is no longer wet in spots, 10-15 minutes.
7. Place the baking sheet on a cooling rack until the pecans are completely cool.

Do Ahead: Nuts can be made 2 weeks ahead. Store in airtight container at room temperature.

Serving suggestion tag and gift tags for this recipe on page 76.

Delicious for snacking or gift giving
they're incredibly easy to prepare.
Package these tasty morsels in cellophane
bags, cute little jars, or gift tins and add
to your stash of holiday gifts.

This cozy acorn squash is roasted to perfection and accented with candied pecans and goat cheese. Welcome to your new favorite side dish.

Roasted Acorn Squash with Candied Thyme Pecans

The autumn flavors of acorn squash paired with tangy goat cheese and sweet pecans makes for a crowd favorite dish. The finishing drizzle of balsamic vinaigrette creates a sensational blend of flavors.

Squash

1. Preheat oven to 425°F.
2. In a large bowl, toss sliced squash, olive oil, salt and pepper until well coated.
3. On a rimmed baking sheet, arrange coated squash in a single layer. Roast until golden brown and tender, 20-25 minutes. Let cool slightly.
4. Transfer to a serving platter. Scatter candied pecans and goat cheese over top of squash.

Vinaigrette

1. In a small bowl, whisk together olive oil, balsamic vinegar and honey until emulsified.
2. Drizzle over squash and serve.

SERVINGS: 6-8

SQUASH

2 medium acorn squash, (1 1/2 lbs. each) seeds removed and cut into 1/2-inch slices
1/4 cup olive oil
kosher salt to taste
black pepper to taste
1 cup candied pecans
2 oz. goat cheese, crumbled (about 1/3 cup)

VINAIGRETTE

1 Tablespoon olive oil
1 Tablespoon balsamic vinegar
1 teaspoon honey

Cheese Board with Candied Thyme Pecans

SERVINGS: 6-8

1/2 cup candied thyme pecans, chopped

2 Tablespoons dried apricots, chopped

1 Tablespoon parsley, chopped

2 4-oz. goat cheese logs or 1 10-ounce goat cheese log

A cheese board is my go-to appetizer for everything from a casual get together to more formal entertaining. It's incredibly simple to pull together your favorite selection of cheese with refrigerator and pantry items you have available. A cheese board with accompaniments gives your guests the option of mixing and matching flavors as they see fit.

It's ideal to provide 5 different types of cheese, about 1/2 ounce of each cheese per guest, but I often create cheese boards with as little as two types of cheese. Your selection can include a range of milk types, flavors and textures. I often opt for a hard cheese, a semisoft cheese, a rich creamy cheese and a pungent cheese. I assemble the cheese by cutting into wedges and strips that can easily be eaten. When it comes to accompaniments, well I just can't have enough of them. A few will suffice, but indulge if you must. For those that prefer their cheese and accompaniment assembled together, I've included an easy recipe for a candied pecan goat cheese roll.

SELECT YOUR CHEESE

Hard Cheese: Asiago, aged Gouda, Manchego, Parmigiano-Reggiano

Semisoft Cheese: Farmers, Fontina, Havarti, Monterey Jack, Mozzarella, Provolone, Muenster

Rich Creamy Cheese: Brie, Burrata, Camembert, Chevre

Pungent Cheese: Epoisses, Gorgonzola, Maytag Blue Cheese, Roquefort, Stilton, Taleggio

ADD ACCOMPANIMENTS

apple slices	dried fruit	olives
berries	fruit compote	pear slices
celery	fruit paste	pepper jelly
chutney	grainy mustard	pistachios
candied thyme pecans	honey	radishes
dark chocolate	honey comb	walnuts
	Marcona almonds	cornichons

BREAD AND CRACKERS

tortas de aceite	seed crackers	baguette
lavash	herb crackers	sour dough
	whole grain bread	

Candied Pecan Goat Cheese Roll

1. In a shallow dish, toss pecans, apricots and parsley together.
2. Roll log of cheese in nut mixture until well coated. Tightly wrap in plastic wrap. Repeat with remaining cheese and refrigerate.
3. Let sit at room temperature for 20 minutes before serving whole or sliced.

Do Ahead: Cheese rolls can be made 2 days ahead. Keep chilled. Let sit at room temperature for 20 minutes before serving whole or sliced.

Serving suggestion tag and gift tags for this recipe on page 76.

Holiday parties and many other life events warrant a cheese board. Raid your pantry and refrigerator and easily create and epic cheese board for any gathering.

Don't bother cooking your own chicken for this salad when a juicy, supermarket rotisserie chicken will do. Toss in candied thyme pecans for a touch of sweetness and the perfect amount of crunch.

Chicken Salad with Candied Thyme Pecans

You're going to love the sweet pop of flavor from the candied nuts and grapes in this easy chicken salad. Yes, a store-bought rotisserie chicken will make a flavorful salad that can be served in a variety of ways. This salad is potluck perfect on a bed of greens, and can also be served as an appetizer by scooping into mini bell peppers or lettuce cups. For a heartier option, serve with your favorite croissant or rolls. I often mix it up and create a crowd pleasing platter for casual entertaining.

1. In a large bowl, stir together mayonnaise, lemon juice, salt and pepper.
2. Add chicken, grapes and onions, and mix until well combined.
3. Add the pecans and mix until combined.
4. Serve on a bed of lettuce, scooped into mini bell peppers, lettuce cups or on your favorite bread rolls.

Do Ahead: Chicken salad can be prepared 2 days ahead; cover and chill. Mix in candied thyme pecans just before serving.

Serving suggestion tag and gift tags for this recipe on page 76.

SERVINGS: makes 6 cups

3/4 cup mayonnaise

1 Tablespoon lemon juice

1/2 teaspoon kosher salt

1/2 teaspoon fresh cracked black pepper

1 rotisserie chicken, deboned and coarsely chopped

1 cup red seedless grapes, halved

1 cup green onions, chopped

1 cup candied thyme pecans, coarsely chopped

This incredibly easy recipe for candied pecans is perfect for holiday gift-giving! Surprise your friends and family with this tasty treat by packaging in cellophane bags, jars or tins. They'll enjoy candied pecans as an appetizer for parties, a topping for cakes or stirred into oatmeal and yogurt. Create a lovely hostess gift by making the recipe for a Pecan Goat Cheese Roll. Tuck it into a basket with artisanal crackers and a beautiful spreader knife. This will be everyone's favorite treat!

CANDIED PECAN GOAT CHEESE

ROLL

A YDELICACIES.COM RECIPE

CANDIED PECAN GOAT CHEESE

ROLL

A YDELICACIES.COM RECIPE

CANDIED PECAN GOAT CHEESE

ROLL

A YDELICACIES.COM RECIPE

WITH CANDIED THYME PECANS

CHICKEN SALAD

A YDELICACIES.COM RECIPE

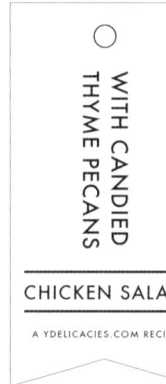

WITH CANDIED THYME PECANS

CHICKEN SALAD

A YDELICACIES.COM RECIPE

WITH CANDIED THYME PECANS

CHICKEN SALAD

A YDELICACIES.COM RECIPE

CANDIED THYME PECANS

Serving Suggestions

- MIX INTO CHICKEN SALAD FOR
A SWEET AND SAVORY FLAVOR
- SERVE AS AN ACCOMPANIMENT ON
A CHEESE BOARD
- CHOP AND ADD TO YOUR BAKED
SWEET POTATOES
- TOSS INTO SPINACH SALAD OR COLESLAW
- ADD A HANDFUL TO ICE CREAM

A YDELICACIES.COM RECIPE

CANDIED THYME PECANS

Serving Suggestions

- MIX INTO CHICKEN SALAD FOR
A SWEET AND SAVORY FLAVOR
- SERVE AS AN ACCOMPANIMENT ON
A CHEESE BOARD
- CHOP AND ADD TO YOUR BAKED
SWEET POTATOES
- TOSS INTO SPINACH SALAD OR COLESLAW
- ADD A HANDFUL TO ICE CREAM

A YDELICACIES.COM RECIPE

TAG INSTRUCTIONS

1. Photocopy or scan tags onto cardstock. Alternately, go to **Ydelicacies.com** and search **"printables"**.

2. Open scanned/photo-copied file or website file and print tags onto cardstock.

3. Use scissors or craft knife to cut out tags.

4. Fold and crease Candied Thyme Pecan Serving Suggestion tags. Punch out hole through both thicknesses of card stock with a hole punch. For Candied Pecan Goat Cheese Roll and Chicken Salad with Candied Thyme Pecans tags punch out hole in single thickness of card stock.

5. String decorative ribbon or twine through the hole and tie tag to edible gift.

6. Holiday Biscotti

Fragrant spices and chewy cranberries make this biscotti recipe scream all things holiday. Biscotti is a twice baked treat that will fill your home with the most exquisite holiday aroma. It can be stored for weeks in tins making this available as a shareable sweet that is perfect for dunking in your morning coffee or your afternoon Vin Santo. If you're in need of a dessert be sure to try the Holiday Biscotti Semifreddo where you'll fold these tasty morsels into a rich and creamy frozen treat.

Holiday Biscotti

SERVINGS: 26-28 biscotti or about 60 cantucci

1 1/2 cup all-purpose flour
1/2 cup sugar
1 1/2 teaspoons baking powder
1 1/2 teaspoons ground ginger
1 teaspoon ground cinnamon
1/2 teaspoon ground nutmeg
1/2 cup walnuts
1/2 cup dried cranberries
1 teaspoon orange zest
2 eggs, beaten
2 Tablespoons water
1 teaspoon molasses
2 teaspoons sprinkling sugar, or granulated sugar

Holiday biscotti is a twice baked cookie that is very dry and perfect for dunking. The dry texture makes it ideal for storing batches of make-ahead gifts. In Italy cantuccini, a mini version of this cookie, is eaten after a meal dipped in Vin Santo wine. Across the pond, people eat biscotti dipped in coffee or espresso. Whether you bake biscotti or the mini cantuccini size, dipping it in coffee or Vin Santo is always a perfect way to end a meal.

1. Preheat oven to 300°F. Line a baking sheet with parchment.
2. In a large bowl, whisk the flour, sugar, baking powder, ginger, cinnamon and nutmeg together. Add the walnuts, cranberries and orange zest and stir to combine.
3. Make a well in the center of the dry ingredients and add the eggs, water and molasses. Using a fork, stir the eggs, water and molasses together and begin incorporating the dry ingredients. When dough begins to form, finish mixing the dough by hand until all the dry ingredients are incorporated.
4. Shape dough into a 10 x 2-inch log and place on the prepared baking sheet (for cantucci, shape dough into two thinner 10-inch logs and bake 30-35 minutes). Sprinkle the top with sprinkling sugar. Bake until a tester inserted into the center of the log comes out clean, 45-50 minutes.
5. Let cool for 5 minutes and slice into 1/4 inch slices. Place slices on the baking sheet cut side down. Return to oven and bake for 7 minutes. Flip slices, return to oven and bake for 5 minutes longer. Biscotti may be slightly soft in the center, but will harden as they cool. Transfer to wire racks to cool completely.

Do Ahead: Completely cooled biscotti can be stored in metal tins or airtight containers for up to one month.

Serving suggestion tag and gift tags for this recipe on page 86.

This flavorful and festive holiday biscotti is perfect for cookie exchanges and gift baskets. They're delicious shared with house guests over a cup of coffee or a glass of Vin Santo.

This no-churn frozen dessert with a light texture is both dramatic and easy, making it the perfect dinner party dessert.

Holiday Biscotti Semifreddo

Impress your friends and family with this make-ahead, creamy dessert. It's a no-churn treat so an ice cream machine isn't required. You'll discover that crushed holiday biscotti adds the perfect amount of crunch to the frozen, silky texture.

1. Line the loaf pan with plastic wrap leaving enough to overlap the sides. Set aside.
2. In a large bowl using an electric mixer, beat cream until stiff peaks form, 3-5 minutes. Gently stir in the condensed milk and salt just until combined. Fold in 1 cup of the biscotti.
3. Transfer the mixture into the lined loaf pan and smooth the top. Freeze until firm, about 4 hours. Serve semifreddo slices topped with the remaining crushed biscotti.

Do Ahead: Biscotti can be prepared up to 1 month ahead. The semifreddo can be prepared up to 1 week ahead and stored in freezer until ready to serve. Top with remaining crushed biscotti when serving.

SERVINGS: 8-12

2 cups heavy whipping cream
3/4 cup sweetened condensed milk
1/8 teaspoon kosher salt
1 1/2 cups crushed biscotti, divided
Special equipment: 9x5-inch loaf pan

Your edible gift stockpile should include baskets filled with holiday biscotti, a pound of coffee and a mug. For a unique hostess gift try cantucci, the smaller size biscotti, paired with a bottle of Vin Santo. Whether your gifting biscotti with coffee or Vin Santo, these hand formed treats are sure to delight year after year.

TAG INSTRUCTIONS

1. Photocopy or scan tags onto cardstock. Alternately, go to **Ydelicacies.com** and search **"printables"**.

2. Open scanned/photo-copied file or website file and print tags onto cardstock.

3. Use scissors or craft knife to cut out tags.

4. Fold and crease Holiday Biscotti Serving Suggestion tags. Punch out hole through both thicknesses of card stock with a hole punch. For Holiday Biscotti tags punch out hole in single thickness of card stock.

5. String decorative ribbon or twine through the hole and tie tag to edible gift.

HOLIDAY BISCOTTI

Serving Suggestions

- DIP IN HOT CHOCOLATE OR COFFEE
- DIP IN DESSERT WINE SUCH AS VIN SANTO
- CRUSH AND TOP ICE CREAM

A YDELICACIES.COM RECIPE

HOLIDAY BISCOTTI

Serving Suggestions

- DIP IN HOT CHOCOLATE OR COFFEE
- DIP IN DESSERT WINE SUCH AS VIN SANTO
- CRUSH AND TOP ICE CREAM

A YDELICACIES.COM RECIPE

7. Sweet and Savory Scones

When you want a quick baked treat for brunch, tea or easy weekend mornings, scones fit the bill. Enjoy their tender texture paired with butter, preserves or lemon curd. Savory scones can be served with soup or salad for a satisfying meal. These scones don't transform into other dishes, but I often share them as edible gifts. The following pages do offer three make-ahead options that will keep you minutes away from these deliciously baked treats! If you're in need of a gift idea, scones are easily packaged with a jar of preserves for a hostess gift to be enjoyed the morning after the party.

2 1/2 cups all-purpose flour,
plus extra for flouring
surface

1/4 cup sugar, plus extra for
topping

2 teaspoons baking powder

1/2 teaspoon baking soda

1/2 teaspoon salt

1 Tablespoon lemon zest

3/4 cup (1 1/2 sticks) unsalted
butter, chilled

1 cup fresh blueberries

3/4 cup sour cream

2 Tablespoons milk, plus more
for brushing on top

1 teaspoon vanilla

1 large egg

Lemon Blueberry Scones

This recipes ease of preparation made me a scone fan. Three make-ahead options allow my family to enjoy fresh baked scones with coffee or tea when the cravings hit.

1. Preheat oven to 375°F. Line a baking sheet with a silicone mat or parchment.
2. In a large mixing bowl, whisk together flour, sugar, baking powder, baking soda and salt. Add the lemon zest and toss to coat with flour. Grate the butter into the bowl and toss to coat with flour. Blend butter into the dry ingredients by rubbing between your fingers until the mixture is crumbly.
3. Add the blueberries and gently toss to coat with the crumbly flour mixture. Make a well in the center of the flour mixture.
4. In a small bowl whisk together the sour cream, milk, vanilla and egg. Pour into the flour well, and use your hands to gently combine just until the dough comes together. Do not over mix as this will result in tough scones.
5. For 8 large scones: On a floured surface, pat the dough into a 1-inch thick disc (8-9 inches in diameter). Transfer the disc to the prepared baking sheet. For 16 mini scones: On a floured surface, divide the dough into two equal pieces. Pat each piece of dough into a 1-inch thick disc (about 5-inches in diameter each). Transfer the discs to the prepared baking sheet.
6. Brush dough with milk and generously sprinkle with sugar. Dust a knife with flour and cut each disc into 8 wedges, keeping the wedges touching each other in a disc shape. Bake in the preheated oven until golden brown, large scones 25-30 minutes, mini scones 20-25 minutes. Cool on baking sheet for 5 minutes. Transfer to a cooling rack to cool completely.
7. Serve with lemon curd, butter, clotted cream, whipped cream, or your favorite jam.

Do Ahead:

BAKED OPTION: Scones can be made 1 day ahead. Cool completely before storing covered at room temperature.

REFRIGERATED OPTION: The prepared dough can be formed into a disc, sealed in plastic wrap and refrigerated overnight. Brush with milk, top with sugar, cut and bake as directed the following day.

FROZEN OPTION: The prepared disc of dough can be frozen whole or cut into wedges. Simply wrap in plastic wrap and place in a re-sealable freezer bag. Scone dough will store in a freezer up to 2 months. When you're ready to bake, place scones on baking sheet and allow them to sit at room temperature for 30 minutes, brush with milk, top with sugar and bake.

Baking Instruction tag and gift tags for this recipe on page 96.

Yes, scones are best when served fresh from the oven. However, they're delicious a few hours later or even the next morning, making this a great hostess gift idea when packaged with honey butter or jam.

Do Ahead:

BAKED OPTION: Scones can be made 1 day ahead. Cool completely before storing covered at room temperature.

REFRIGERATED OPTION: The prepared dough can be formed into a disc, sealed in plastic wrap and refrigerated overnight. Brush with milk, top with fresh cracked pepper and bake as directed the following day.

FROZEN OPTION: The prepared disc of dough can be frozen whole or cut into wedges. Simply wrap in plastic wrap and place in a re-sealable freezer bag. Scone dough will keep for up to 2 months. When you're ready to bake, place on baking sheet and allow to sit at room temperature for 30 minutes, brush with milk, top with fresh cracked pepper and bake as directed.

Savory scones are a nice change from cornbread or rolls. Served them with soup or salad for a satisfying meal. Enjoy them for breakfast with butter, jam or a drizzle of honey for an unexpected flavor pairing.

Asiago & Sun Dried Tomato Scones

We usually think of scones as sweet, not savory. This recipe is packed with shredded Asiago cheese and sun dried tomatoes for a rich, tender scone. Serve savory scones whenever you would serve cornbread or rolls... you'll be glad you did.

1. Preheat oven to 375°F. Line a baking sheet with a silicone mat or parchment.
2. In a large mixing bowl, whisk together flour, sugar, baking powder, baking soda, salt and cayenne pepper. Grate the butter into the bowl and toss to coat with flour. Blend butter into the dry ingredients by rubbing between your fingers until the mixture is crumbly.
3. Add the cheese and sun dried tomatoes and gently toss to coat with the crumbly flour mixture. Make a well in the center of the flour mixture.
4. In a small bowl whisk together the sour cream, milk, and egg. Pour into the flour well, and use your hands to gently combine just until the dough comes together. Do not over mix as this will result in tough scones.
5. For 8 large scones: On a floured surface, pat the dough into a 1-inch thick disc (8-9 inches in diameter). Transfer the disc to the prepared baking sheet. For 16 mini scones: On a floured surface, divide the dough into two equal pieces. Pat each piece of dough into a 1-inch thick disc (about 5-inches in diameter each). Transfer the discs to the prepared baking sheet.
6. Brush dough with milk and top with fresh cracked pepper. Dust a knife with flour and cut each disc into 8 wedges, keeping the wedges touching each other in a disc shape. Bake in the preheated oven until golden brown, large scones 25-30 minutes, mini scones 20-25 minutes. Cool on baking sheet for 5 minutes. Transfer to a cooling rack to cool completely.
7. Serve with soup or salad. Enjoy for breakfast with butter, jam or a drizzle of honey for an unexpected flavor pairing.

Baking Instruction tag and gift tags for this recipe on page 96.

SERVINGS: 8 large or 16 mini scones

2 1/2 cups all-purpose flour, plus extra for flouring surface
1 Tablespoon sugar
2 teaspoons baking powder
1/2 teaspoon baking soda
1/2 teaspoon salt
1/4 teaspoon cayenne pepper
3/4 cup (1 1/2 sticks) unsalted butter, chilled
4 oz. Asiago cheese, grated
1/3 cup sun dried tomatoes in oil, well drained
3/4 cup sour cream
2 Tablespoons milk, plus more for brushing on top
1 large egg
fresh cracked black pepper

Make someone's holiday even sweeter with a basket filled with handmade scones. Scones can be packaged in a ready-to-bake disc of dough allowing your recipient to enjoy fresh-from-the-oven scones. If you choose to gift freshly baked scones, bundle with honey, preserves or lemon curd in a beautifully presented basket. Whether sweet or savory, scones can be served any time of day, making them a perfect gift giving treat.

LEMON BLUEBERRY **SCONES**
A YDELICACIES.COM RECIPE

LEMON BLUEBERRY **SCONES**
A YDELICACIES.COM RECIPE

LEMON BLUEBERRY **SCONES**
A YDELICACIES.COM RECIPE

ASIAGO & SUN DRIED TOMATO **SCONES**
A YDELICACIES.COM RECIPE

ASIAGO & SUN DRIED TOMATO **SCONES**
A YDELICACIES.COM RECIPE

ASIAGO & SUN DRIED TOMATO **SCONES**
A YDELICACIES.COM RECIPE

LEMON BLUEBERRY SCONES

Baking Instructions

- PREHEAT OVEN TO 375°. PLACE DOUGH ON A BAKING SHEET LINED WITH PARCHMENT.

- BRUSH DOUGH WITH MILK AND GENEROUSLY SPRINKLE WITH SUGAR. DUST A KNIFE WITH FLOUR AND CUT DOUGH INTO 8 WEDGES.

- KEEP WEDGES IN DISC SHAPE, AND BAKE IN PREHEATED OVEN UNTIL GOLDEN BROWN, 25-30 MINUTES.

- COOL ON BAKING SHEET FOR 5 MINUTES. TRANSFER TO A COOLING RACK TO COOL COMPLETELY. SERVE WITH LEMON CURD, BUTTER, OR JAM.

A YDELICACIES.COM RECIPE

ASIAGO & SUN DRIED TOMATO SCONES

Baking Instructions

- PREHEAT OVEN TO 375°. PLACE DOUGH ON A BAKING SHEET LINED WITH PARCHMENT.

- BRUSH DOUGH WITH MILK. DUST A KNIFE WITH FLOUR AND CUT DOUGH INTO 8 WEDGES

- KEEP WEDGES IN DISC SHAPE, AND BAKE IN PREHEATED OVEN UNTIL GOLDEN BROWN, 25-30 MINUTES.

- COOL ON BAKING SHEET FOR 5 MINUTES. TRANSFER TO A COOLING RACK TO COOL COMPLETELY. SERVE WITH SOUP OR SALAD FOR A SATISFYING MEAL. ENJOY THEM FOR BREAKFAST WITH BUTTER, JAM OR A DRIZZLE OF HONEY FOR AN UNEXPECTED FLAVOR PAIRING.

A YDELICACIES.COM RECIPE

TAG INSTRUCTIONS

1. Photocopy or scan tags onto cardstock. Alternately, go to **Ydelicacies.com** and search **"printables"**.

2. Open scanned/photo-copied file or website file and print tags onto cardstock.

3. Use scissors or craft knife to cut out tags.

4. Fold and crease Scones Baking Instruction tags. Punch out hole through both thicknesses of card stock with a hole punch. For Lemon Blueberry Scones and Asiago & Sun Dried Tomato Scones tags punch out hole in single thickness of card stock.

5. String decorative ribbon or twine through the hole and tie tag to edible gift.

8. Glitter Cookies

These are the Glitter Cookies I mentioned in the introduction. As a young girl, the holiday season always included Mrs. Irma Ramos' glitter cookies. Each Christmas, she would bake my family a batch of glitter cookies until I began baking them myself when I was 12 years old. So began my childhood obsession with edible gifts.

My daughters have enjoyed glitter cookies throughout their childhood, and they've transformed them into a decadent treat called a Mookie Cookie. It starts by sandwiching two glitter cookies together with raspberry jam, and ends with a dip in melted chocolate for an incredibly rich treat. I hope your family enjoys these cookies as much as my family has enjoyed baking and gifting them throughout the years.

Glitter Cookies

SERVINGS: 3 dozen cookies

2 cups all-purpose flour
1/2 teaspoon cream of tartar
1/2 teaspoon salt
1/2 teaspoon baking soda
1/2 cup butter, softened
3/4 cup powdered sugar
1/2 cup granulated sugar
1/2 teaspoon vanilla extract
1/2 teaspoon almond extract
1 large egg
1/2 cup vegetable oil
red sugar crystals
green sugar crystals

It wouldn't be Christmas without a few batches of glitter cookies. Their delicate texture makes for a much appreciated gift idea that will have everyone asking for more. The dough freezes beautifully making this a great prep-ahead treat during the hustle and bustle of the holiday season. I must admit, I make these cookies year-round by simply changing the color of the sugar crystals. I dip the dough in pastel colored sugar crystals for a delightful spring cookie, and multi-colored sugar crystals for birthday celebrations. Don't let their simple shape and easy-to-prepare recipe fool you. These cookies are crisp yet tender, and yes, they're addictive.

1. In a medium bowl, whisk together flour, cream of tartar, salt, and baking soda. Set aside
2. In a large mixing bowl, using an electric mixer on medium high speed, blend the butter, powdered sugar, granulated sugar, vanilla extract and almond extract until light and creamy. Scrape down the sides of bowl.
3. With the mixer on low speed add the egg. Add the oil in a steady stream until blended. Stop the mixer and scrape down the sides of the bowl.
4. With the mixer on low speed slowly add the dry ingredients just until combined.
5. Cover and chill dough for 4 hours, but preferably overnight.
6. Preheat oven to 350°F. Line a baking sheet with parchment or a silicone mat.
7. Fill a small bowl with red sugar crystals, and another small bowl with green sugar crystals.
8. Use a small spring-release scoop or a Tablespoon to scoop dough and shape into 1-inch size balls.
9. Dip each ball into the red or green sugar crystals, and gently press down. Place on prepared baking sheets 2-inches apart with sugar crystals side up. Bake until the bottom is light golden brown, 10-12 minutes. Let cool slightly on baking sheet, then transfer to a wire rack and cool completely.

Gift tags for this recipe on page 106.

Do Ahead: Glitter cookie dough can be prepared and stored in the freezer in re-sealable freezer bags for up to one month. Thaw in refrigerator overnight, scoop into cookies and bake. Individual cookie dough balls can be shaped, dipped in sugar crystals and frozen on a baking sheet. Transfer frozen cookie dough balls into re-sealable freezer bags and store up to 1 month in freezer. Place frozen cookies on baking sheet, and thaw at room temperature for 30 minutes before baking.

Glitter Cookies are the first edible gift I can recall baking. I began sharing these wrapped on disposable plates, and I now share them in apothecary jars, acrylic trays and gift tins.

Do sweet treats get any better than this sugar cookie-raspberry-chocolate combo? I think not.

Mookie Cookies

These cookies are named after my daughter's nickname, Mookie. She imagined this cookie-jam-chocolate combination, and I created it. It remains a favorite treat with both of our daughters. During their high school years, we often prepared a batch and package them as birthday gifts for their friends. They're also adorable individually wrapped in glassine bags. It's so characteristically like our daughter to reimagine the humble glitter cookie into an indulgent treat. Enjoy! (See resources on the A Few of My Favorite Things page for glassine bags, page 13)

1. Line a baking sheet with parchment, waxed paper or a silicone mat.
2. Spread about 1 teaspoon of jam on the bottom of a cookie. Gently press the bottom of another cookie against the jam. Repeat until all of the cookies are sandwiched together.
3. Place chocolate in a heat-proof glass or metal bowl. Set over a saucepan of simmering water. The simmering water should not touch the bottom of the bowl. Stir until the chocolate is melted and smooth.
4. Dip half of each sandwich cookie into the melted chocolate. Place on prepared baking sheet.
5. Refrigerate to set the chocolate, about 30 minutes. Alternately, let the chocolate set at room temperature, about 2 hours. Mookie cookies should be served within 1 day as the jam tends to soften the cookies. Store at room temperature in an air-tight container.

Gift tags for this recipe on page 106.

SERVINGS: 18 Mookie Cookies

1 recipe Glitter Cookies (page 100), made with Rainbow Sparkling Sugar baked and cooled
1/2 cup raspberry jam (with or without seeds)
12 ounces milk chocolate

Instead of hitting the stores for last-minute gifts, spend your time making edible gifts. There's something spectacular about a delicious, homemade gift. This Glitter Cookie recipe is perfect for the first-time cookie baker, and you can easily package your cookies in cellophane bags, boxes or tins. Use the resources on the A Few of My Favorite Things, page 12, for packaging ideas.

For the more adventurous baker, prepare Mookie Cookies that can be bundled together or individually wrapped in glassine bags for the perfect co-worker gift. Whether you bake Glitter Cookies or Mookie Cookies, they're sure to become a holiday staple in your home.

GLITTER COOKIES — A YDELICACIES.COM RECIPE

GLITTER COOKIES — A YDELICACIES.COM RECIPE / MOOKIE COOKIES — A YDELICACIES.COM RECIPE

TAG INSTRUCTIONS

1. Photocopy or scan tags onto cardstock. Alternately, go to **Ydelicacies.com** and search **"printables"**.

2. Open scanned/photo-copied file or website file and print tags onto cardstock.

3. Use scissors or craft knife to cut out tags.

4. Punch out hole in single thickness of card stock.

5. String decorative ribbon or twine through the hole and tie tag to edible gift.

MOOKIE COOKIES — A YDELICACIES.COM RECIPE